TRUMP

COLORING BOOK

COLOR TEST PAGE

CPAC

DONALD
TRUMP
FRAGRANCE

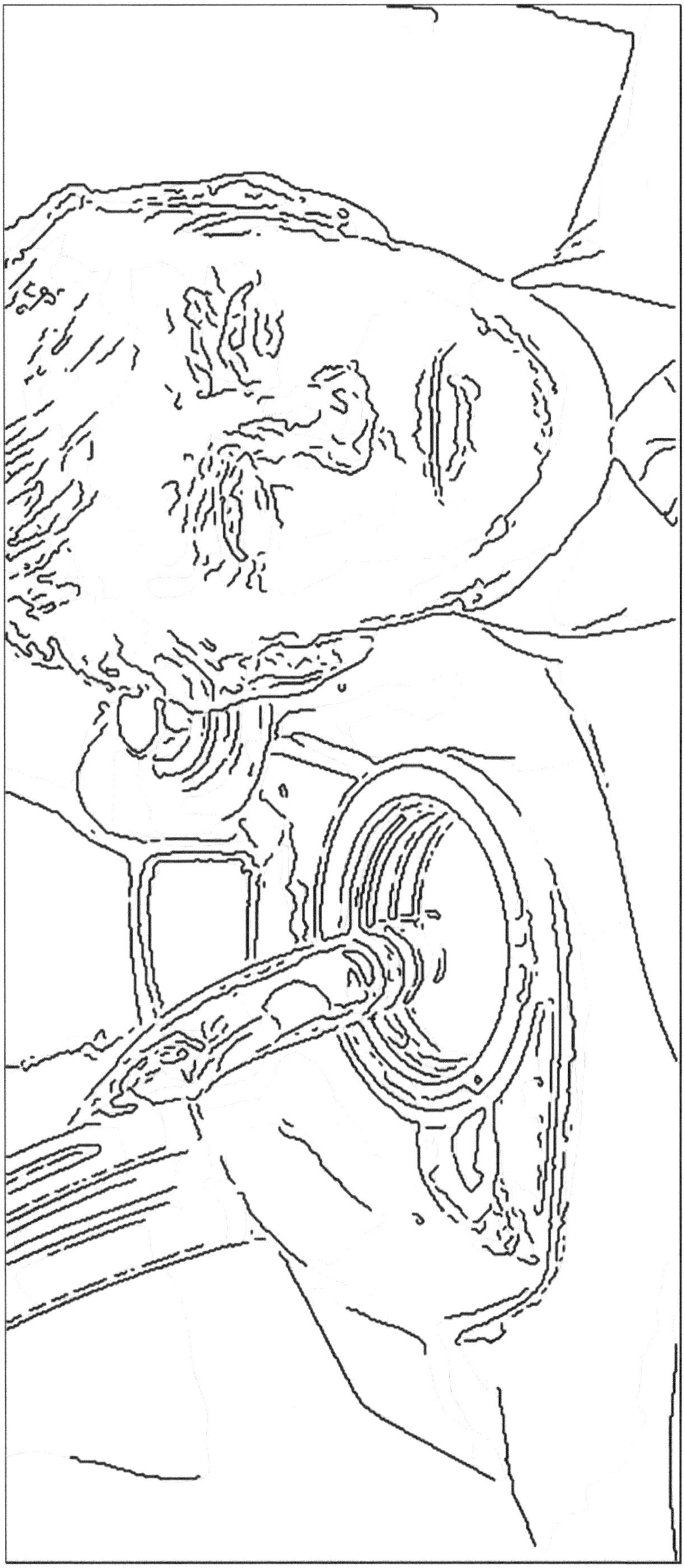

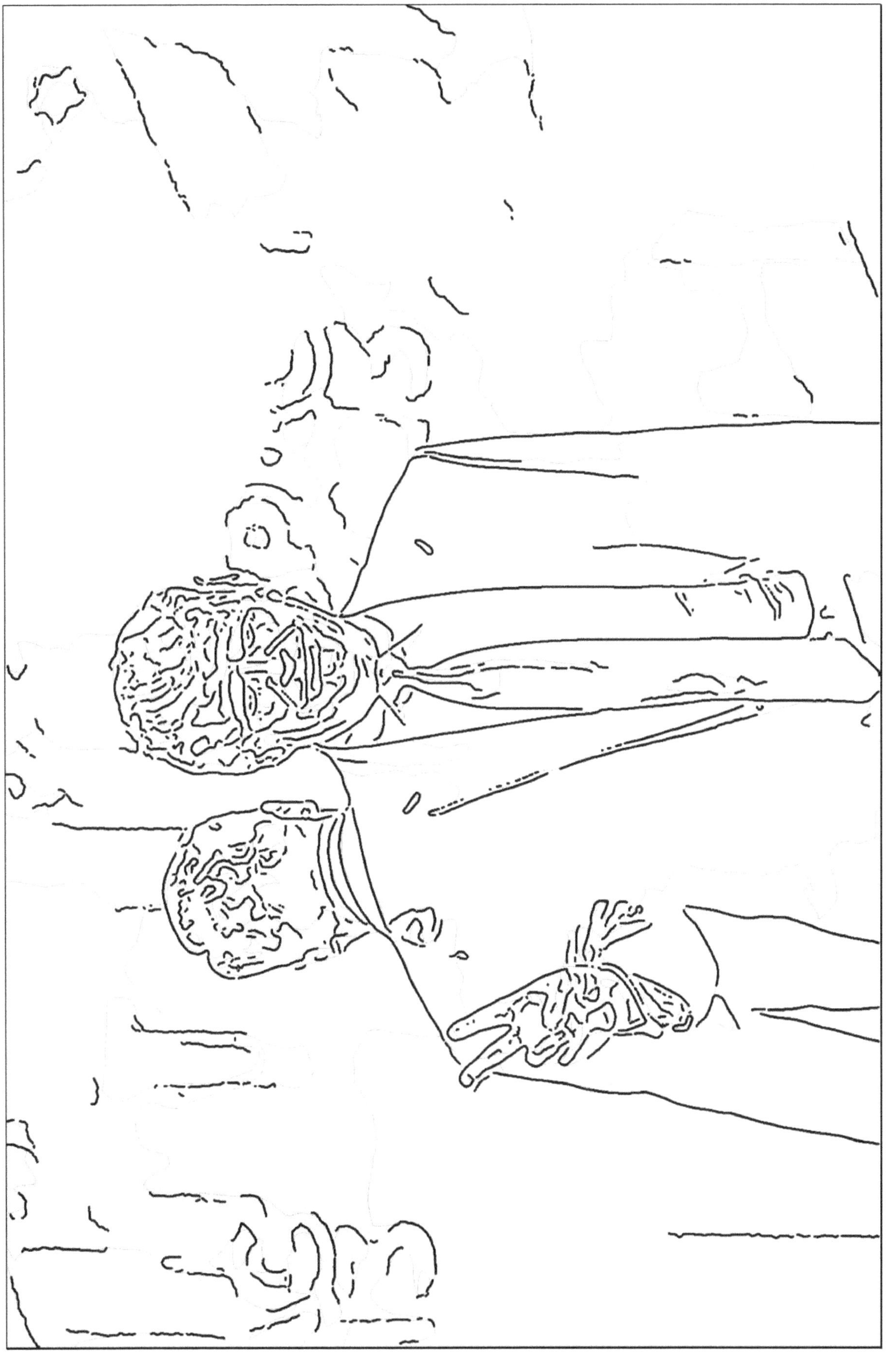

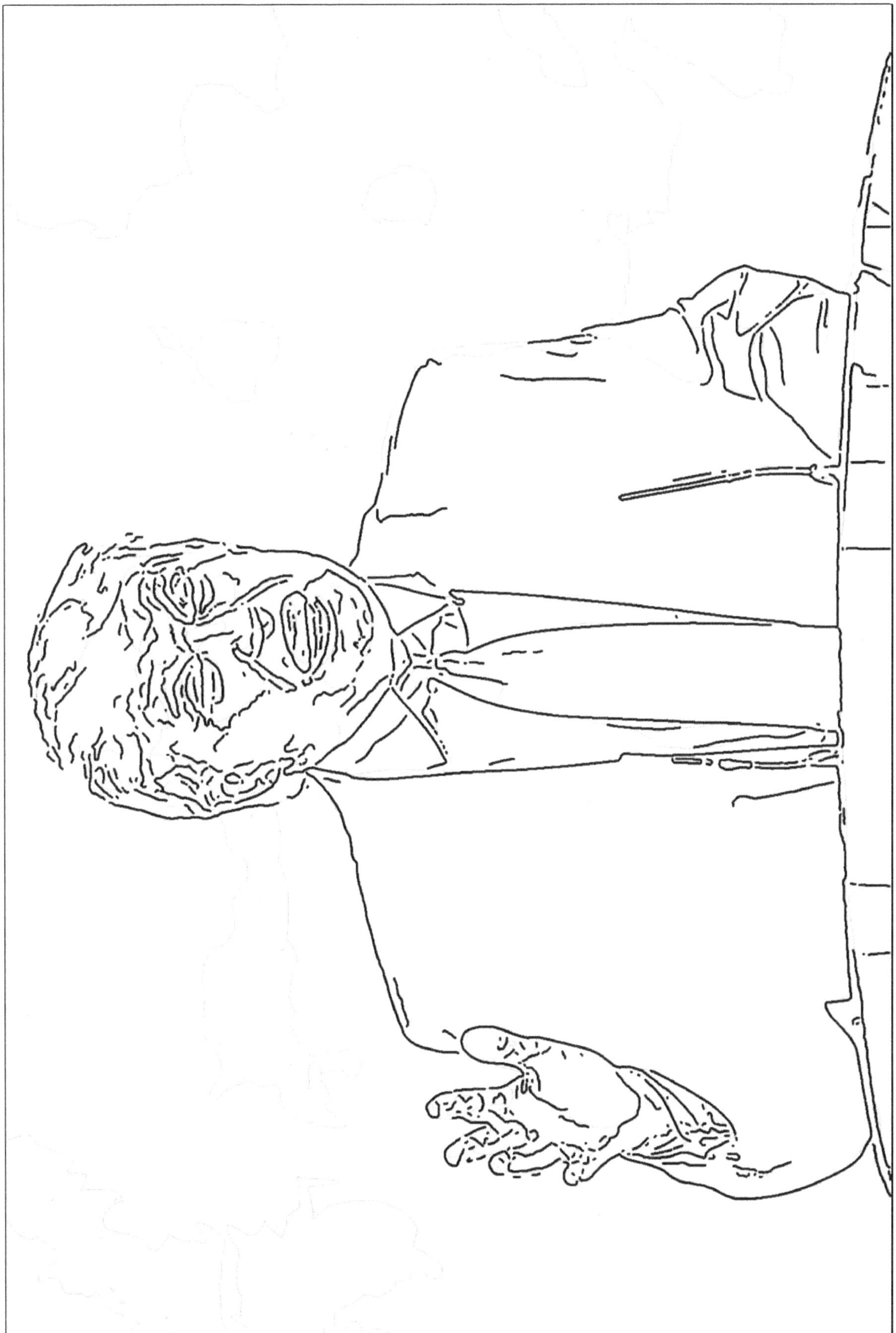

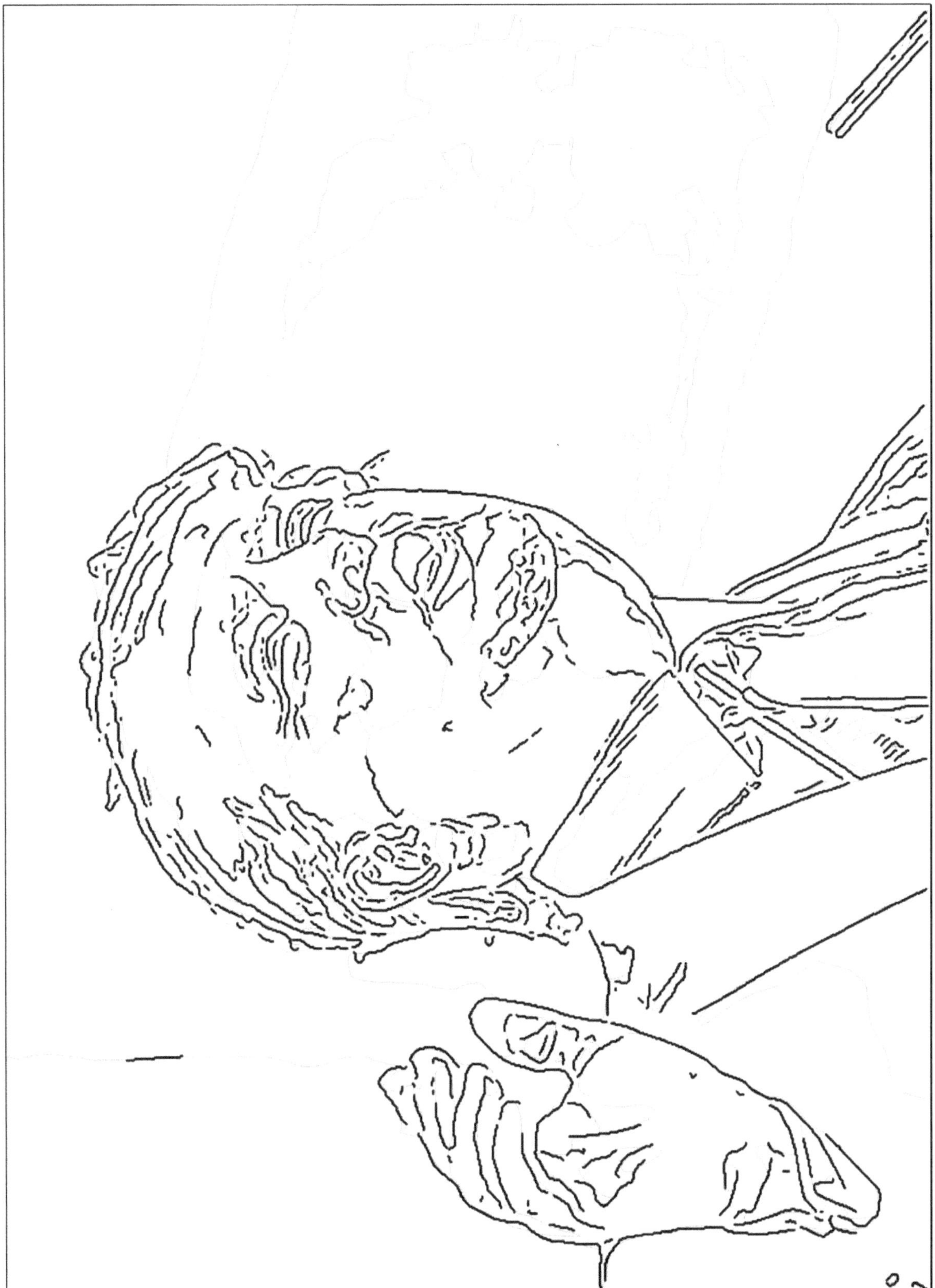

#FITN
REPUBLICAN LEADERSHIP SUMMIT

TRUMP
TRUMP

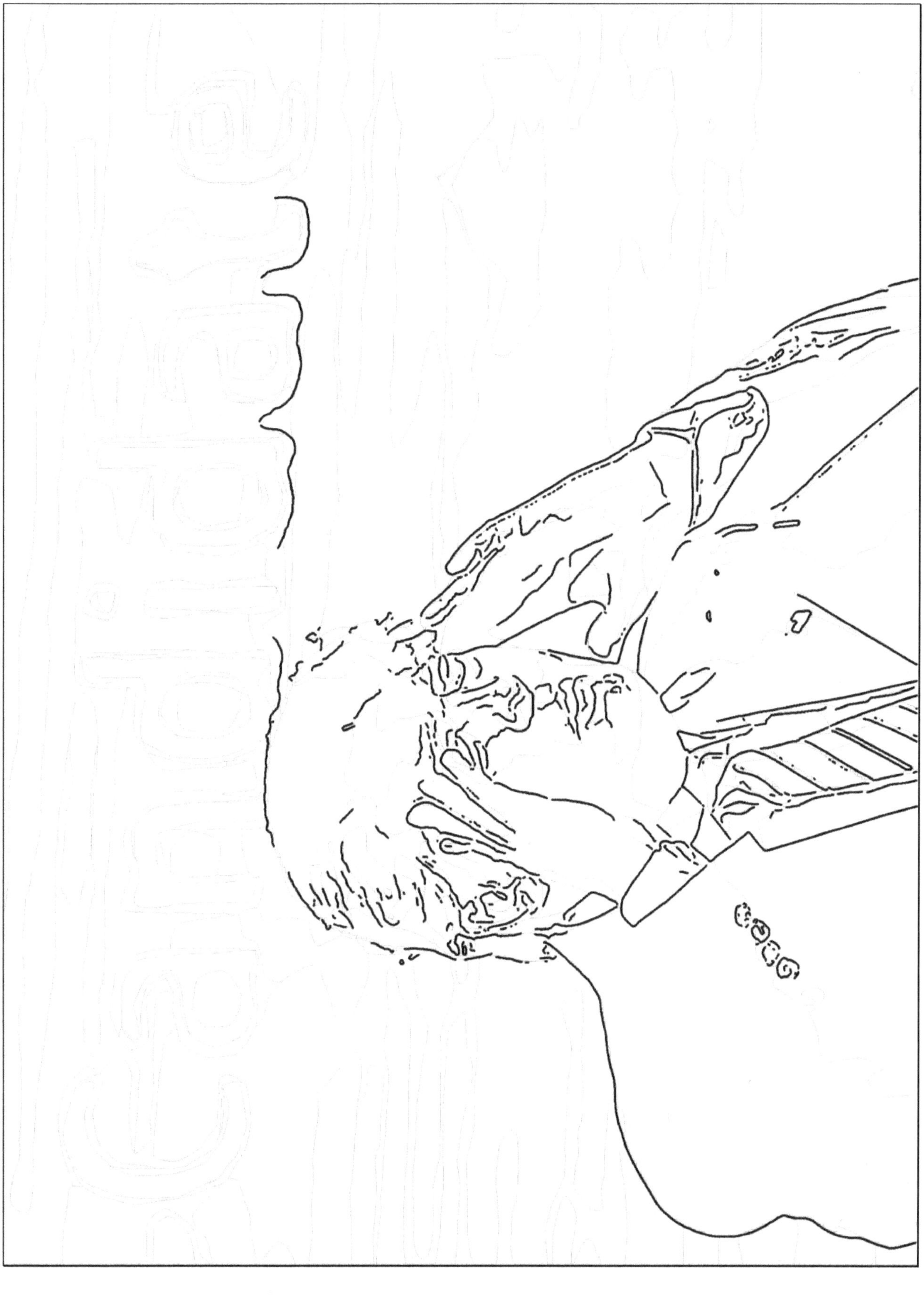

TRUMP

www.ingramcontent.com/pod-product-compliance
Lightning Source LLC
Chambersburg PA
CBHW081127280526
45787CB00007B/3010
9781535000437